ISBN 978-0-259-53110-4
PIBN 10200186

This book is a reproduction of an important historical work. Forgotten Books uses
state-of-the-art technology to digitally reconstruct the work, preserving the original format
whilst repairing imperfections present in the aged copy. In rare cases, an imperfection in
the original, such as a blemish or missing page, may be replicated in our edition. We do,
however, repair the vast majority of imperfections successfully; any imperfections that
remain are intentionally left to preserve the state of such historical works.

Bugle Calls

Awake, Educate, Agitate, Act!

Prose & Verse

" **H**E who will hear, to him the clarions of the battle call. How they call, and call, and call, till the heart swells that hears them. Strong soul and high endeavor, the world needs them now. Beauty still lies imprisoned, and iron wheels go over the good and true and beautiful that might spring from human lives."—Progress and Poverty.

By Benjamin Wood,

Author of "The Successful Man of Business."

New York: Brentano's.

Dedicated to my young daughter
Beatrice Mignonette Wood.

"I KNOW that the world, the great
    big world,
    From the peasant up to the king,
Has a different tale from the tale I
    tell,
    And a different song to sing.

"But for me—and I care not a single
    fig
    If they say I am wrong or right—
I shall always go in for the weaker
    dog,
    For the under dog in the fight."

A Table of the Contents.

THE PREFACE.

THE PREFACE.

The Preface.

THIS appeal to the workingman for organization, harmony, and unity is the outgrowth of a sympathetic feeling nourished into life and activity through beneficial results experienced by the firm with which the author is associated, S. N. Wood & Co., San Francisco and New York, in its transformation from a Non-Union to a Union establishment.

THE work is an indication of this firm's sentiments for trades unions, and has for its motive a desire to weld the employer and employee into a better and more lasting relation. This we believe can only be accomplished through fair wages, shorter hours, pleasanter and more healthful surroundings and through a Union Label imprinted on all commodities manufactured by the hands of labor.

THE author enters no deeper into the sociology and economics of the problem. All he desires is justice for all; and even though his remedy prove unavailing and another succeed he will feel more than delighted to have his single object realized.

PRIOR to the entrance of our firm into the field of unionism, there existed among its respective members the same aversion and antipathy for Unions as at present exist with other merchants and manufacturers.

W E were firmly impressed with the theory that Unions should not exist, that they destroyed the inalienable rights of citizens, and arrayed the laborer against the manufacturer and capitalist.

W HY, then, this change of heart? you may rightly ask. And we answer, not through any mercenary motive, but because the veil of darkness has been lifted from our eyes and we see and understand the principles of unionism and the justice of its policy and polity.

F OR many months Mr. Herman Robinson, organizer for The American Federation of Labor, and Mr. Henry White, General Secretary of the United Garment Workers of America, worked arduously endeavoring to influence our firm to be thoroughly unionized, with Union Cutters, Union Tailors, Union Salesmen. We considered the proposition from all sides, and hesitated in making a change from a certainty to an uncertainty. There was a tinge of skepticism in our reception of the proposals; we feared that grim specter termed a " Strike."

THAT we were at last converted is an acknowledgment that our former opinions on this question were wrong, that we had enveloped ourselves in the fog of our own class prejudices and blinded ourselves with a false impression. Thanks are therefore due to the above-mentioned representatives of Labor for their indefatigable energies in not permitting prejudice to derange our mind or to suppress the feelings of

our heart. We have been con-
vinced that there is nothing to fear
from Labor, provided the employer
is satisfied to have right triumph
over wrong.

SINCE our association with trades
unions, we can merely affirm that we
have had with them no differences,
no disputes, no strikes. Our workingmen perform their duties with
zeal and energy, feeling that they are
not underpaid or overworked. We,
in turn, feel that we are receiving
value for value given, and that the
difference paid in wages and reduction of hours over Non-Union establishments is more than offset through
skill in labor and economy in different directions. Combined with
that, we are having better work-
manship than ever before, and rest

content that our patrons, our families, and ourselves are protected, so far as in our power lies, against the infectious and contagious diseases of the sweatshop.

INTRODUCTION.

Introduction.

THE author has not endeavored to analyze sociology, psychology, or any other " ology," nor has he consciously alluded to wealth in terms other than of fairness. Capital is a pretty useful article when we have it. Bacon says, " Believe not much them that despise riches, for they despise them that despair of them."

No conflict is recognized as raging between Capital and Labor, though it is acknowledged that a condition exists which brings poverty to some and riches to others, and for this a remedy is suggested.

Many a literary license has been taken to present this work in a clear and concise manner so that it will appeal directly to the laboring element. Should what is to follow be somewhat peppery in places, the plea of charity must be the excuse for what is, at worst, merely the personal equation of the pen.

Let us be honest with ourselves. Instinct prompts every man to preserve his life, and, if it is threatened by circumstances, he acts with a strong desire to protect it. We should strive, therefore, to give free play to every interest of man and not to aim to live on the fruits of others' labors. The nearer we approach justice and equity, the more advanced grows our civilization; where Labor receives a just share of what it produces, there we find prosperity and contentment. If the working classes are prosperous, they are able to pay good prices for the commodities of the different products of the world. If robbed of prosperity, with scarcely sufficient to live, they can only purchase little, and that of the coarsest and poorest quality.

LET us consider the situation: Poverty is a relative term. It is not so very hard that one is poor as compared to those who are rich in overabundance, but what is hard is that the poor should have so little when measured by the simplest necessities of life. There is such a thing as absolute poverty which does not require the contrast with luxury to breed discontent. But when this contrast is ostentatiously thrust upon the notice of the helpless poor, discontent grows into anarchy. Where one man lives in a palace and the other has not even a hovel for his abode; where one man has the finest of wearing apparel, and the other is scantily covered, even by rags; where one man feasts on the rarest delicacies, and the other starves without crumbs, it is there that we have the compost which quickens into life the poisonous fungi of social disintegration. The conditions of national ruin are hunger, cold, and nakedness. Poverty begets ignorance, ignorance begets servility, and servility is that disposition which serves him who pays the least. Fairer wages and shorter hours can better these conditions. B. W.

Bugle Calls.

Look Forward to the Day.

IT is with a more than surface feeling for my kind that I take up the old problem of "man's inhumanity to man" and attempt to solve one of its manifold phases. It is not with the rose-colored glasses of poetic imagination, but with the clear lens of converging induction, that I look forward to the time when the present tendencies of civilization shall meet and blend in the kindling focus of common interest, and when every man shall feel that the rights not only of his brother man but of every living creature are as sacred as his own.

NOTHING affords me greater
pleasure than to pay honor and
homage to the trinity of human
rights: life, liberty, and the pursuit
of happiness; nothing affords me
greater peace of mind than the belief that, through the influence of
the Union Label, all will be merged
into the unity of human aspiration, "The Common Brotherhood
of Mankind."

SLOWLY, but more surely than
observers in contracted spheres are
apt to recognize, are we growing toward a realization of equal rights
and equal opportunities for all. Men
are not thinking entirely of themselves, nor are they armor-plated
against the sorrows of their fellow-
man. The desire of men is to be
free, and it is felt that none can be

free where some are slaves; the man who is in danger of want, or even in constant dread of it, is not a free man himself, and his condition, like that of decaying fruit, threatens the soundness of his neighbors. Whatever of oppression comes to one, soon or late is felt by others.

OPPRESSION creates fear: fear of want, fear of starvation, fear that what we own to-day will not be ours to-morrow, fear of public opinion, of private opinion. The editor fears to print the facts; the minister to preach the truth. The air grows miasmatic with the gloom born of the germs of injustice, and fear and despair spread like panic and infection.

LIVING in continual dread, continual cringing, continual fear, weakens the individual in every respect.

Mind is magnetic and attracts to itself whatever is free; the more we open our doors and give opportunity for fear to enter, the more we give cause for fear to come in.

THE speech of Patrick Henry in the Virginia Convention of 1775 is an outcry against injustice. Its sentiment now, as in the past, permeates the atmosphere with magnetic force. Its thought will forever travel onward. Thousands of miles away, and centuries hence, from millions of tongues shall be heard the sentiment which he so eloquently expressed: " Is life so dear, or peace so sweet as to be purchased at the price of chains and slavery? Forbid it, Almighty God! I know not what course others may take, but as for me, give me Liberty or give me Death!"

WE are surrounded with such oppression at present. It is a condition, not a theory, which confronts us. The rich grow richer, the poor poorer. The employer exacts more, and pays less. The cardinal doctrine of democracy, " Equal rights for all, special privileges to none," is but an evanescent dream, vanishing into vapor. The principle, however, is not lost; it shall not be lost! We cannot permit it to be lost! The flame of liberty must never be extinguished. The force of that heat and that aspiration of true democracy must and will forever live. It will absorb and consume material interests; it will combine with our other spiritual thoughts and thus, through the co-operation of unseen elements, will result in a new solidarity. And we believe that this will center around the theory of " The Union Label."

"THE Song of the Shirt" is humming in our ears and appearing in our dreams; it recalls the grim specter " Hard Times," the ghost-like apparition of low wages and dear living. That epoch-marking song demands that the toiler must be housed, fed, and clothed.

> "Oh! men with sisters dear,
>   Oh! men with mothers and wives,
> It is not linen you're wearing out,
>   But human creatures' lives!"

THE purpose of this work is not to class the aspiration for increase of wealth among evil desires, nor to disparage the merits of the millionaires who have acquired their possessions by the exercise of their wit and shrewd business faculties.

The pursuit of wealth is a duty, not alone to oneself and to one's family, but to mankind at large.

IT is not necessary, however, to permit wealth to be our master; let us rather make it our servant and use it as a lever for lifting us to something better and greater, for serving mankind, equalizing wages, endowing colleges, hospitals, libraries, churches, and museums. In fine, let us promote thereby all worthy institutions that conduce toward the elevation and betterment of humanity. Wealth should never dominate, control, nor gain such complete influence over us as to own us body and soul. It is the part of wisdom to appreciate what true living implies and to hold in mind the fact that mere dollars will not and do not produce happiness. Though we have riches, we can only eat so much, drink so much, clothe ourselves and house ourselves; more than that we cannot do.

THE amassing of wealth is not the ideal of life and its aim, or the real object of our existence. There should be a keener appreciation of the higher purposes and pleasures of life than to view it thus narrowly or sordidly. Money is but a subordinate means to afford the gratification of higher aims and tastes and to minister to our needs and those of our dependents.

"We must ever think as we strive for gold,
That a dead man's hand can't a dollar hold,
We may tug, and toil, and pinch, and save,
And we'll lose it all when we reach the grave."

LET it not be said of us when we die that we left a sealed paper wherein was written and bequeathed three legacies, "We owe much, we have nothing, we give the rest to the poor;" but let it be spoken of us that we gave to the poor what is the most priceless bequest, a gentle word, a kind look, and an encouraging smile; that we endeavored to dissipate the disappointment arising from oppression by the ready fraternity of our extended hand.

LET us in particular leave a name that will survive the wreck of mortality, by offering our mite of assistance to those who are chained to long hours and anchored to small wages, by guiding those who are sailing in a light skiff through a tortuous channel, beset with rocks on all sides and driven hither and thither by the swirling current into an unknown sea. Such a record should be the object dear to our heart, and the dream of our ambitions. Endeavor, therefore, to promote and advance the welfare of trades unions and the universal adoption of the Union Label on everything and for everything.

Do not pass through life without doing some good. The story is told of a king of Persia who, conversing with two philosophers and his vizier, asked, "What situation of man is most to be deplored?" One of the philosophers replied that it was old age, accompanied with poverty; the other, that it was to have the body oppressed with infirmities, the mind worn out, and the heart broken by a series of disappointments. The vizier, however, replied that he knew a condition far more to be pitied. "It is that," said he, "of him who has passed through life without doing good, and who, unexpectedly surprised by death, is sent to appear before the bar of the Sovereign Judge of all."

LOOK forward to the day when no truly intelligent man will be satisfied with his own full-fed condition while millions of his fellow-men are hungry and naked; when the ideal man will be he who does not grasp everything within reach or turn a deaf ear to those who suffer; when everyone will feel that the millennium does not mean the lion lying down with the lamb, the latter having an inside berth.

LOOK forward to the day when the earth will be greener, the skies brighter, and the sun shine forth with all its warmth on the Temple of Labor.

"PLANT not, but eradicate the thorn that grows in your partner's pathway." The bestowment of friendly acts can rob wealth of its strength, extract the bitter from the cup of sorrow, and open wells of gladness in many waste places.

> *" Little deeds of kindness, little words of love,*
> *Make this world an Eden like to that above."*

EVERY heart requires sympathy, and is a receptacle for it. "A kind word falls from the lips like oil upon the troubled feelings of the human breast." No flower is as fair as that sympathy which springs from the heart, and no fragrance as sweet as that which is odorous with generosity.

A Key to the Problem.

THE dawn of the twentieth century ushers in an era in which inequity shall be overthrown and justice shall govern.

My writings on this subject are but a mere spark of the huge smoldering fire of discontent in the world; were I not to take the matter up many others surely would. There are multitudes of sympathizers with the cause of humanity; many who desire to render life cheerful for all; to make the air balmy; the sky clear; the trees greener; the flowers more beautiful, and the sun, moon, and stars brighter. There are many who are desirous of striking a chord of benevolence that shall echo and resound throughout the world, a hymn of harmonious humanity. But no great deed or reform was ever created suddenly, any more than a fruit tree produces fruit suddenly; it takes time to blossom, to bear fruit, and then to ripen it.

THE universe means better by humanity than some think. The toiler must not treat the world as his foe, nor try to extort its benefits and rewards by approaching it like a highwayman. Create sympathy through kindness. Create strength by unity. Live up to the sentiment expressed by Benjamin Franklin when signing the Declaration of Independence, " We must all hang together, or assuredly we shall hang separately."

ALL intelligent minds will co-operate in this solution, regardless of differences of wealth, creed, or position; such differences will no longer raise an artificial wall of separation between social ranks and classes.

"*That man may last, but never lives,*
Who much receives, but nothing gives;
Whom none can love, whom none can thank,
Creation's blot, creation's blank."

"DO for your neighbors all the good you can." "If you do good, good will be done to you." "He that watereth shall be watered." "He that plants thorns must never expect to gather roses."

SEAL the doom of small wages and long hours with the verdict of death; both deserve it. Both were doomed from the very beginning of their birth. The forces of evolving civilization are fatal to them. We are moving out of that decadence when men lived like fishes, the great devouring the small; the worm has turned.

WHAT we call money gaining in its broad sense is not moneymaking in its true sense, but money transferring without any sense. It is a process of slave-making; of turning into the pockets of the one that which is rightly earned by the brains or the hands of others.

IT is far from my desire to imply or have it inferred that employers must turn over their entire earnings to the employees, for this system of co-operation can never be perpetuated since the employee does not share in risks or losses. But it is no more than just when an employee earns through his skill five dollars a day that we pay him five dollars. If less is paid him, he is robbed of the difference between what he receives and what he is worth. This difference is transferred to the employer's pocket, as the meed of the master who, under our system of industrial warfare, profits by the protection of might as against the enforcement of right.

THE pecuniary reward which men receive for their services is so absurdly disproportionate to the intellectual power that is needed for the task and also to the toil involved, that men cannot rely upon their pursuits as a protection from money anxieties; they are underpaid and overworked. This evil must be remedied.

THE system of industrial warfare must be stopped. Competition must not be stifled by such devices; the enlisting of the best services with exaction of the most and payment of the least. Such conditions are industrial warfare pure and simple, not industrial competition. Competition is rivalry under conditions of fair play, not where wolves devour the lambs. Industrial competition is that competition where every man has an equal show; where wages are uniform and hours of labor are agreed upon. Different conditions are industrial warfare and industrial crime, whereby the rich grow richer, the poor poorer; the poor man receiving no justice, the rich man all favors.

SINCE the prevailing conditions as to hours of labor, rates of wages, and employment of children of a tender age are so dissimilar and disadvantageous to industrial competition that they seriously threaten the prosperity of the laboring element and of those manufacturers who believe in shorter hours and fairer wages, the toiler should look forward to the formulation and enactment of national legislation to determine the conditions under which they shall work. There is an old adage, "Chickens will come home to roost." So likewise our wrongs to others must come back and fall upon ourselves. If the employer, in order to compete with his rival-employer, reduces wages to the lowest possible degree, that action produces the slavery of the employee. Congressmen and legislators must see the consequences of such acts and help to pass other laws that will raise our Government up to the highest plane of humanity.

THE conditions under which one shall work and receive his pay are fair subjects for the care and attention of the Government, to the end that right and justice shall characterize the dealings of citizens one with another. The toilers or wage-earners constitute so large a portion of the body politic as to entitle them to the fullest safeguarding of their interests. Uniform or universal Labor laws would work the greatest measure of good for all classes.

THE Labor question at present occupies a very different position from that which it occupied generations ago when the question consisted solely of the proposition: How can wages be raised or the working hours per day reduced?

IT now touches fundamentally upon the toiler's interest in society, how he shall receive wages enough to enable him to become a political, a social, and a moral factor in the community. It is now a question of sociology, of how can society develop in the very best way so that all men shall receive something of these things in this life which make for culture and education.

EVER since certain tribes from Central Asia wandered westward and settled in Central Europe, searching for better conditions; ever since Christopher Columbus discovered this great American Continent, there has been this feeling of unrest and discontent, of longing for refinement for advancement, for education, and for higher civilization.

THE very lifeblood in our veins is the heritage of those characters who thousands of years ago longed for a better condition, for a better land. This unrest, this discontent that impels men always and ever to seek better conditions, is natural and legitimate. We should not crush that divine spirit of unrest which makes the world as it is, and gives us whatever civilization exists. We should rather contribute to the sum of knowledge that which shall mold the mind and sharpen it into some effective force which shall further better human conditions.

LET us improve our industrial systems. One manufacturer cannot pay high wages and run his mill a reasonable number of hours in competition with his rival-manufacturer of the same line of goods if the latter underpays his men and overworks them. We should understand what is to be done, and then set about to do it with all our might.

PLACE yourself upon record as an advocate for well-paid, independent labor; for justice and equity. Demand that every man who toils and produces be compensated in exact proportion to the value of his labor and for the benefit he bestows upon others by his skill and efforts.

UPHOLD Trades Unions, for they aim primarily to ameliorate the condition of the employee and not to antagonize the employer; they purpose to make known and understood the needs and shortcomings of all organized craftsmen, and to put forth intelligent and continual effort to improve their standing and efficiency.

LET there be one keynote that will harmonize the discord between poorly paid and well-paid toil, between Union and Non-Union products, skilled and unskilled labor. That keynote is A Union Label—A Union Flag.

THE Union Label is the efficient force for good in the struggle for labor's amelioration and the working-man's emancipation. It is the emblem of well-paid, independent Labor; the badge of Honesty; the symbol of Fair Dealings; the token of True Brotherhood, and the open and avowed enemy of the Sweatshop. It stands for wholesome and sanitary conditions as opposed to prison and child labor. This emblem is to the workingman's cause what the Stars and Stripes are to our country. It stands for a new Declaration of Independence. Wherever it waves and to whomsoever it dips in salutation it cries out for "Justice and Equity!"

What Does It Signify?

PURITY and justice are stamped on the face of the Union Label. The Label conforms to a strict performance of moral obligations, and its freedom from any sinister motive is reflected in the condition of well-paid workmen, well-fed children, and happy homes. Healthful conditions surround those who rally around that banner, and through its influence is felt and recognized the truth that human life is of greater moment than gain of gold.

IT is the seed of a new life, the life of brotherhood, justice, mercy, and love; though the cradle of a new issue, there is in it that which will in time revolutionize the conditions of labor; the time will never come when we shall follow its corpse to the grave; for nothing can perish that embodies the principles of sobriety, truth, justice, and morality, of "Vigilance not Violence."

THIS Label is the battle-emblem of the laboring classes; it will be carried throughout the world wherever there is a struggle for bread for life and the triumph of Right over Wrong. It is but a tiny piece of paper, a little rag of linen, but through the power of the seal imprinted thereupon, it is metamorphosed into a weapon of defense, an instrument with which the noblest and bravest will fight until justice liberates the sons of toil who now rest in durance vile.

THE Label points the road to a higher ideal, a higher standard of social, intellectual, and moral well-being. It preaches the Gospel of Unionism, champions the cause of Labor, promotes its welfare, and will in time secure for it shorter hours and better wages.

LABOR'S hope of deliverance from oppression rests upon its ability to rally round one common standard.

A S long as workingmen continue to buy Non-Union-made goods, just so long will respect for them be less and merchants continue to handle that class of goods whose existence proclaims Labor's servility.

THE laborer's cause cannot be destroyed by external foes, its ruin can only be wrought from within. The hope of the toilers, the prayer of all our people for justice, lies in the

Label; stand by it, and it will stand by you.

WHAT does this Label signify? It signifies that a fellow-unionist has been over the battlefield and fought his way against oppression. It points the road to Union Labor, guides the buyer, and shows the wage-worker where to find friends among employers.

IT signifies that human life is becoming more highly prized in the production of human commodities than mere profit; it warns you that by patronizing a firm who does not uphold it, you assist in building up the business of a tyrant who extracts a fortune from the drudgery and degradation of his fellow-men. Therefore, create the demand. Ask for a Union Label wherever you go, whatever you purchase. Even though you are aware that a Label is not on the market, nevertheless demand it. Demand governs supply.

THE more Union Labels, the more Union purchases. The more Union purchases, the more Union men. The more Union men, the more strength obtained, the more power wielded. Harmony pervades your ranks, less discord arises; you gain wisdom, and wisdom gets you justice.

WISDOM will give you a voice in shaping the affairs of our Government. By uniting under one banner, one Union Label, your strength is concentrated and the force at your disposal is irresistible.

CALL for force, demand force, and then seek for wisdom to apply it. The thought ever going in a current from you will be a force acting on other minds, and as real in such action, though unseen, as the pressure of your arm against a door.

MONOPOLIES and powerful corporations are begotten by the originators meeting together and talking the matter over. By communication and interchange of opinion with those of your like order of thought you will find that the ideas which for years have been knocking at your doors are living truths and not vain notions and fancies.

THE more you direct your minds toward a realization of the highest ideals, the more constructive force will you accumulate and generate to develop into organized power, just as the larger the boiler, the more force is generated and the greater number of machines moved thereby.

THE very existence of the toilers depends upon their power of combination. The hope for the future improvement in the condition of Labor rests upon the intelligence and loyalty of the whole Labor movement. Labor's powers and energies must, therefore, be directed toward the unification and solidarity of the organized workers. The cry for liberty, for shorter hours, for better wages, must not be a hypocritical vaporing, but a clear conception of what Labor proposes to do.

PURPOSE to keep everlastingly asking for a Union Label. If an employer conducts his business without the Label, give him an object lesson on the purchasing power of

Labor by showing him that there are other merchants more to your liking.

A IM to do no one wrong by uniting and federating in this manner, but establish justice for all. People as a rule are wedded to custom and are slow to comprehend the necessity for a change. Divorce them from custom, and do it systematically.

S UCCESS, individually or collectively, is attained only by continuous, well-directed, intelligent, and energetic work; failure results from apathy. If every Union man will try to make himself worth as much to the Union as the Union has been of value to him, he will not go to his grave without ever having a luxury; nor will he deform himself, or be food for others, devoured by his fellow-man. Stop to consider that it is the Union man who, in purchasing the products of a Non-Union firm, puts it in the power of that firm to compel others to follow his example. The toiler cannot expect the respect and appreciation of the public when he has no respect or appreciation for himself,

THE ills you bear are the results of conditions within your own control. You are responsible for injustice, for want, for crime, and wretchedness caused by your not understanding the economic law by which you are controlled. Do not blame the capitalist. He means no harm; you harm yourself unknowingly. Learn your lesson, then apply the remedy; an empty stomach can be filled and a naked back clothed through the influence of the Union Label.

THE demand must first come from the working classes, from the oppressed, from the hungry, from the downtrodden, from men who despair and women who weep, not from the merchant. The toilers must tell what the Union Label stands for. They must make known to the purchasing public that in buying any commodity with a Label thereon, they are not becoming a partner to an institution which degrades humanity for profit alone. They must tell that a Label on a garment, on a box of cigars, on a loaf of bread, or a piece of printing, signifies that no little children set fingers thereupon ; that no germs of smallpox, typhus fever, or leprosy is scattered thereabout ; that no convicts and no degraded specimens of humanity put their life's blood into marketable goods.

A UNION Label on a box of cigars signifies that the cigars are not the coffin-nails of Death, but were made by first-class workmen devoted to the advancement of the moral and intellectual welfare of the craft, not by coolies, by Mongolians, diseased with smallpox and yellow fever. Were smokers only to see the pestholes where Non-Union cigars are made, no legislation or Label would be required to eradicate the evil. See APPENDIX—Hon. Theodore Roosevelt.

T HE Label on a loaf of bread signifies that the bread was baked in a clean bakeshop, not in one of those dark ratholes whose filth the mind can hardly conceive ; not in hovels of human habitation where men, women, and children, making their shops their sleeping abodes, are herded together like so many cattle; mingling with chickens and dogs, with waterbugs, cockroaches, and other insects; living and baking in low, tumbled-down shanties or cellars, where the ceiling fairly touches the occupant's head, where flues are defective, where the steam condenses and falls in drops on the baker's brow, and from the sweat of that brow into the dough of your bread.

PICTURE squalid, filthy rooms, surcharged with the foulest odors and laden with diseased germs; conceive of poor drainage, defective plumbing, the lack of the simplest means of ventilation, the breathing of air utterly unfit for respiration. The employer steals the sunlight from humanity as the great oaks rob

the smaller trees ; the stronger ani-
mal devours the weak; everything is
at the mercy of selfishness and greed,
inequality and injustice.

SUCH labor is the rich man's food
and the poor man's poison. We support the drainage of the swill barrels
of the industrial world, instead of
patronizing clean, wholesome conditions; yet if we do not come to the
relief of those poor, ignorant, helpless creatures, their want will be ex-
asperated into crime. See APPEN-
DIX—Factory Inspector's Fourteenth
Annual Report.

THE Label on a hat or pair of
shoes signifies that the shoes or hats
were made by Union men in Union
factories, not in prisons. It is a living evidence that the toilers have
worked under sanitary conditions

and have received living wages. It strikes out with a blow from the shoulder for shorter hours and more healthful conditions, and invites the co-operation of all persons who believe in good work, good wages, and absolute fairness.

ON clothing it signifies that to the workingman has been shown a newer and broader outlook; that he scents fresh air where before he was stifled; that he has become a new creature, braver, nobler, more cheerful and more contented; that the world for him is not a narrow edifice with the cope of Heaven alone for his roof, his way lighted only by the lamps of the stars, but that the spot wherein he works is a haven of rest; the path on which he walks a track of light; that he is not robbed of that completeness of life which goes to make a human being, nor deprived of the full measure of his person—physical, mental, and social.

IT teaches the workingman that industrial sovereignty is the sovereignty of manhood, that sovereignty protests against filth, and poisonous dust, bad air, foul odors, and crowded workshops; that it rescues the soul from abortion and signs it with the seal of American manhood and citizenship; that it recognizes the workingmen as our strength and the very foundation of the nation's greatness.

IT means that it will not permit the cannibalistic manufacturer to devour greedily the flesh and drink the blood of a toiling, groaning, trembling, suffering humanity.

IT means that it will not make them slaves to toil, drudging from early morn till late at night for bare necessaries, with a sense of injustice rankling in their minds, equally for what they have not, and for what others have.

A MAN with a just heart cannot be satisfied until he effects better conditions. It almost makes us ashamed to be well dressed and warm when we see our fellow-men in misery and want, famished, ragged, and shivering.

WHY not rally to their assistance? Shall your heart be as cold as the bodies of these poorly clad garment makers?

HOW can the Union Label ever become a factor of beneficence unless you act consistently and support it? Do you not realize that it is the only safeguard that your garments were made in light, clean, airy workrooms, where sanitary regulations are adhered to, where contagious and infectious diseases are not rampant? Do you not know that the sweatshop is spreading consumption broadcast; that throughout the entire East Side of New York City men, women, and children are huddled together in living apartments, bedrooms, kitchens, and even narrow hallways; that the floors and walls reek with filth, and the inhabitants perhaps have made their beds out of the garments which you now have on your back? Is it not a pleasing reverie—"From the consumptive's back to your back;" garments saturated and impregnated with pathogenic germs of a deadly disease? See APPENDIX—Factory Inspector's Fourteenth Annual Report.

SUCH conditions should arouse your intellect, even though blind madness had deranged your mind.

WAKE up, citizen! You are falling behind. If the foregoing facts are unpalatable it is better they should be known than that you should continue to sleep and dream amidst filth and disease.

THE Union Label is in its formative stage; in the near future it will be the key to the solution of Labor's amelioration. Its influence in this problem will be comparable to the great strength of Niagara, and like unto that great torrent which gains its current from the deep and peaceful waters of the lake from which it issues, so the laboring classes will gain power through the peaceful issue of the Union Label.

FIGURATIVELY speaking, the Label is like a little boy a few months old lying helpless in his cradle with barely sufficient strength to move a muscle, or power enough to hold his milk bottle to his mouth; yet in that feeble youngster we know lie the power and possibilities which twenty years hence may enable him to lift with ease weights that stagger ordinary humanity. All record-breakers were once " mewling " infants.

IF the strength of the Union Label is not proportionately influential and powerful, the fault will be in the indolence, the selfishness, and short-sightedness of the laboring man, for it is evident that the large multitude of toilers will and can emancipate themselves by its wide usage. Therefore, give us a Label for everything we wear, from the sole of our feet to the crown of our head. See APPENDIX—" Union Label."

HAMMER it into our shoes, paste it in our hats; sew it in our wearing apparel. Have the baker bake it in his bread, the painter paint it on his signs, the plasterer plaster it on the walls, the polisher polish it in his metals, the machinist mold it in his engines, the pattern maker fashion it in his patterns. Have the sailor nail it to the mast and the shipwright carve it at the prow. Have Union doctors bow us into the world, and Union gravediggers usher us out.

LET the good work creep on. Though but a hint, a wish, a desire, a demand, that one man scarcely whispers to his neighbor for fear of ridicule, it will grow, according to the laws of nature, to be the voice of an enthusiastic people.

CHARACTERIZE this agitation by uniform decorum and good conduct. Destroy all hypocrisy, all false measures, perverted aims, and low pandering to ignorance and brutality.

L ET it be said that, in this instance at least, the toiler has evinced an honorable eagerness to sacrifice time, means, comfort, and convenience, and to cast aside all petty feelings in a cause which is sacred and beneficial, in a cause which is an inspired evangel of a new religion of humanity.

L ET it be the glory and boast of the dawn of the twentieth century, that all classes have turned their attention to the hardships and perils of our working classes and will do all they can to better their condition.

I F through it all but one atom of good shall be achieved for the workingman; if through it all we shall aid in lessening ever so little the continuous strife between Capital and Labor, it will be a far grander and nobler triumph than ever has been wrung from the complacent charity of the rich by the importunities of the poor.

LET us not covet a single leaf of the laurels that encircle the brow of those who put fetters upon the mind, soul, and body of man, woman, or child. Let us not envy their triumph. Theirs be the glory of carrying it; ours, of having to the utmost of our poor ability resisted it.

WE can safely conclude that if this Union Label, after being incorporated into the woof of our social fabric, shows that it can produce equally good results wherever and whenever it is accepted, it is close to an absolute truth, an absolute solution of the laboring problem.

I TS benefits will come like the appearance of a nearby spring of fresh bubbling water to one well nigh overcome with thirst; like a full burst of moonlight to one staggering in the darkness; like a seed planted in fertile soil which in due season will sprout and bring forth its fruit. They shall give to labor the strength of a giant and impart to his heart the tenderness of a babe.

"*All seems beautiful to me.*
I can repeat over to men and women, You
    have done such good to me I would do
    the same to you.
I will recruit for myself and you as I go;
I will scatter myself among men and women
    as I go;
I will toss a new gladness and roughness
    among them."

T HUS wrote that poet who was so great that he knew no envy, no prejudice; who never boasted that he was higher nor lower than any other man, meeting all on terms of absolute equality, mixing with the poor, the lowly, the oppressed as well as the cultured and rich, a man who said to the outcast, "Not till the sun excludes you will I exclude you." Such conduct begets good will of man for man; we see and feel the sunshine of friendship beaming from the countenance of everyone we meet.

Love Thy Neighbor.

HOW seldom do we pause in the pursuit of happiness to consider wherein it consists. How often do we seek happiness in wealth that, when obtained, debars its possessor from the freedom of living.

GRAY hairs and the winter of old age steal quickly upon us and we look fearfully forward with tearful eyes and sorrowful heart, feeling that death will soon break the chain which binds us to life. It is then we see that the greed for gold has degraded our higher and nobler ideals of life and that the power and supremacy which wealth affords were not worth the fighting for.

IT is then we realize that, just as Jacob rolled the stone from the well to permit the shepherds and their flocks to quench their thirst, so they who use their money in the cause of humanity have opened wells that will send forth the waters of life forever.

> *" Some have too much, yet still do crave;*
> *I little have, and seek no more;*
> *They are but poor, though much they have,*
> *And I am rich, with little store;*
> *They poor, I rich; they beg, I give;*
> *They lack, I have; they pine, I live."*

THOMAS CARLYLE, in his " Past and Present," says, " We have sumptuous garnitures for our life, but have forgotten to live in the middle of them. . . . Many men eat finer cookery, drink dearer liquors, but what increase of blessedness is theirs? Are they any better, stronger, braver? Are they even what they call happier? . . . To whom, then, is this wealth wealth? Who is it that it blesses? Makes happier, wiser, more beautiful, or in any way better? . . . In the midst of plethoric plenty the people perish; with gold walls and full barns, no man feels safe or satisfied."

" *Backward, flow backward, O tide of years!*
I am so weary of toil and of tears,—
Toil without recompense, tears all in vain!
Take them, and give me my childhood again! "

So pleads the toiler as cold and cheerless appears his outlook, with no vivifying influence to cool his fevered brow, no joy to uplift his mind.

As the past, the present, the future, pass before him at a glance, presenting the false colorings of the world, his soul dreads the aspect. Broken in spirit, toiling from day to day for a miserable support, he falls bound in the mighty chains of servitude.

"Let me to-night look back across the span
'Twixt dawn and dark, and to my conscience
* say—*
Because of some good act to beast or man,
* The world is better that I lived to-day."*

A N aged saint once said, that " No man could rightfully define the word Heaven until he stands by a newly made grave ; one may sometimes see more through his tears than when looking through the largest telescope; he who has never wept does not know the value of laughter; he who has not labored and toiled along the hot and · dusty roads does not appreciate the bliss of sitting under the friendly branches of a shady tree."

T HE moral of that story proclaims " Peace, good will toward men."   It teaches that which will contribute to our present comfort as well as our future happiness; it expands our views, strengthens our resolves, and points to Christ's teachings, " Thou shalt love thy neighbor as thyself." And when asked the question, " Who is my neighbor?" it tells the answer expressed in immortal story, " Every-one who needs thy help."

ITS greatest plea is charity. It breathes Christianity and begs us to enter the hut of the poor man and sit down with him and his children, and, if possible, make them con-tented in the midst of privation and hardship. It impresses upon our mind the principles of a just union as of brother and brother, not as of slave and master, and gives us to understand that we should meet man face to face, heart to heart, and hand to hand. We are not independent parts, but compacted members of one great organization — Mankind. All things are implicated in one another, and the bond is holy. Mankind is only another word for humanity.

IF one will picture the mechanics building our huge commercial structures and consider the enormous risk to life in such labor, then weigh the danger, the skill, and the efforts of the workers against the wages they receive, the scales cannot balance.

BEHOLD the brawny blacksmith, the grimy miner, the sweating stoker, the brave engineer, the dauntless sailor, the fearless fire laddie, the pestered conductor, and the frozen gripman!

BEHOLD their labor-stained faces and soiled garments, which are the outward signs of an honest purpose, while their hard hands are the symbols of tender, affectionate hearts. The collier crawls in the underground, the farmer plods along with his hoe, the blacksmith wields his ponderous hammer, and the engineer in his midnight vigils watches the track to save our lives. They all pursue necessary, and therefore honorable callings.

Think for Yourself.

THE toilers pull down the venerable Temple of Justice and Liberty with their own rash hands on their own devoted heads. They demolish the good and increase the evil by closing their eyes to the consequences of their acts. They rush on to their doom, laboring over ten hours a day, and accepting less than a fair day's wages. They give the most, get the least, and yet continue to patronize those who thrive on their degradation—"the Non-Union establishments." The spirit of Trade-Unionism is thus violated by the very men who should certainly be the last to do to others what they would not wish others should do to them.

THE old axiom says, "Where two laborers seek one employer, the employer fixes the price of wages; but where two employers seek one laborer, the laborer fixes the price."

TO make a good argument two things are requisite: first, that the principle itself be sound; secondly, that it corresponds to the fact that it assumes.

THE toilers, to be prosperous, must have two or more employers seek one laborer. This can be compelled through organized power, by every toiler becoming a full-fledged Union man, buying only Union-made products, and demanding that every commodity bear a

Union Label. This course of action means in time that all mechanics will become Union men; the Label is the tool by which the machine can speedily be constructed. "On the Highway of Destiny a man meets no one but himself." Enthusiasm and earnestness are contagious; it is impossible to make others feel a sentiment unless you feel it yourself.

THE working classes must act together. They have in their hands, if they know how to use it, the power of becoming masters of the situation. Self-protection is the end of their political economy. Reason argues that they are sure to be the victims of the misuse of capital, if they are unguarded.

THE Union Label affords protection. It is an instrument of progress, a lever by which the laborers may hope to raise themselves, if they will but exercise a little effort and self-denial.

LIKE every other expedient, the Label is a means to an end, this being the amelioration of labor, shorter hours, fairer wages, and the prevention of any predominance of tyranny by one class over another.

WORKINGMEN, weigh this appeal solemnly; if you feel that you can agree with me, go among your friends and acquaintances and make converts to your ideas. Speak in season and out of season, in public and in private; agitate the problem.

DIVINE Omniscience has implanted within us the principle whereof springs this Label. By it mankind shall develop into other and better conditions. It is the sovereign scepter of Labor, to conquer the traitors to common justice, when all else has failed.

" Decrees are sealed in Heaven's own chancery,
Proclaiming universal liberty,
Rulers and kings who will not hear the call,
In one dread hour shall thunder-stricken fall.

" So moves the growing world with march sublime,
Setting new music to the beats of Time;
Old things decay, and new things ceaseless spring,
And God's own face is seen in everything."

THE toilers must have objects to attain as well as their employers. Why should they be cajoled? Let employers picture themselves in the laborers' place. Let them see themselves as others see them. Sympathy will follow knowledge, and desire to act, sympathy. Not to desire to act under these conditions is but to confess that you have no principle.

Workingmen, the evils you endure are remediable by yourselves. You have dwelt in sties too long, while society lifts up its perfumed hands in horror at your bad taste and enforced low desires. Medicine cannot be made more pleasant through thinking of its taste, so swallow this quickly. You are suffering from a disease termed "Oppression," with but one remedy at hand, and that remedy a panacea, "Education." Is the disease more agreeable than the remedy? Workingmen, pardon my plainness, I mean no offense. I desire to reach your heart, to strike at your conscience, and this can only be done by calling a spade a spade, and the truth the truth.

IT is said, that "A nation's greatness depends not on acres, but upon the education of the people."

ORGANIZED Labor, in order to accomplish permanent improvement, must look to the education of legislators. The first duty of the laboring interests is to fill our halls of legislation with those who understand the true and harmonious relations of Labor and Capital. Distinguish between the true statesman and the demagogue. Demagogues by false legislation have nearly shipwrecked humanity and have occasioned incalculable misery in the world. Corrupt members of representative bodies have for a consideration subserved the purpose of great corporations and capitalists, selling the interests of their constituents; the workingman finally foots the bill by the parings from his wages.

THE Labor problem is a workingman's problem, of him and by him, as well as for him. The capitalist will not seek to solve it for the laborer; the workingman must do it for himself. Legislation is the primary constructive point around which better conditions must center. Instead of begging and trusting to others to legislate for them, the laborers themselves should be properly represented in the legislature; those who are not of you cannot appreciate your true wants or even understand your condition; it is the most complete evidence of indolence and indifference on the part of the laborers that they are not better represented.

WHAT the future of the world is in the workingman's hands is a matter not of fancy but of fact. The laboring class has it in its power to send to Congress those who shall fully represent its interests. A remedy is required. Let it be applied at once so that government may be conducted primarily in accordance with the interests and demands of the laboring party.

ENTER upon the political field in the manner of an evangelist, not to gratify ambition, commercial or political, but to exercise a trust which has been given for the advancement of the human race. Let the workingmen regard every human being as a kinsman and work together for the common brotherhood of mankind. Let them be friends and exponents of the most complete equality to which humanity can attain, compatible with the public good. Let them be faithful workers in the cause of human advancement and strive to better the conditions of the poor and friendless, so as to secure to the great mass of their fellows the just reward of toil. To merge all minds into this one channel cannot fail to result in the good of the whole.

R ACE with your fellow-man, but do not run a foul race; do not treacherously disable your comrade. Run with all your might on the path of right to reach the goal of independence, enlightenment, and progress, and thus keep forever at the head of truly democratic ideas.

WHEREVER you find a law insufficient or ineffective, point out the defect and suggest the remedy.

HAVE your country lead the world in the purity, honor, and justice of its government, the happiness of its citizens, and the high character and ennobling influence of its civilization.

GO forth not as messengers of war but as heralds of humanity. Consider the best means of promoting safety and comfort and contributing generally to the prosperity of our great industrial order.

GET above the clouds. Let the sun of freedom shine for all and the stars of hope illume the entrance of the twentieth century. Laborer or capitalist, we are all the children of one Father—God.

"THE night is far spent, the day is at hand: let us therefore cast off the works of darkness, and let us put on the armor of light. Let us walk honestly, as in the day."

THERE are not two kinds of creatures, nor two kinds of liberty, superior and inferior; nor are there two sorts of men, men with rights inalienable and men with rights alienable. All come into this world on an equality, feeble in body and mind, but with the seed of improvement in both body and mind; therefore progress and intellectual excellence are our duty, our honor, and our interest.

WORKINGMEN, you have a voice in shaping our government —make use of your voting power. Let your vote be the corner stone of the Temple of Justice and Liberty.

FIGHT for your children as well as for yourselves; for your children's children and the unborn millions of people yet to follow. Fight for the women you love, for the children you adore, and for the homes you prize. Send your representatives to Congress pledged to support legislation controlling the hours of labor and the rates of wages. When you have accomplished the grand duty of electing men to office who will promote such movements you can safely, yes proudly, await with patience the certain progress of reform. Use the ballot, it is there for that purpose. Do not permit the ambitious man of wealth to trample on the bodies of thousands, to dethrone justice so as to gain his world. "Unite." The fagot is stronger than its parts.

CONGRESSMAN John J. Lentz, of Ohio, said: "Unorganized Labor is the timid, crouching, servile instrument of Capital, yielding its head and extending its neck to the yoke of the master. Unorganized Labor stands before the American people as a pitiable example of that old saying, that 'necessity knows no law.' They have become so hungry and so naked, that to satisfy their immediate physical wants they are perfectly willing to sacrifice every mental and moral want, not only to themselves, but of their posterity, even to the fourth generation."

THE rapid changes that constantly take place in the methods of production require continual efforts on the part of trade unions to maintain the rights of the laboring element.

ORGANIZED Labor is the promoter of public peace and happiness; where Labor organizations are strongest, strikes are most infrequent. The only hope for the people arrayed against the great aggregations of Capital is in the balancing influence of Labor organizations.

DOCTORS have their associations, lawyers theirs; that which is right with others is not wrong with the workingman. Progress is the law of nature.

WORKINGMEN, you must not stand still, you cannot stand still, you must go forward or backward—which shall it be?

REMEMBER it is not a question of politics, but a question of right or wrong. There must be a legislature ready and willing to inquire into and remedy without fear or favor every abuse of the laboring world, and to represent fully the feelings of all classes. There is a perfectly clear and well-defined meaning to the words "right" and "equality" when applied to the administration of justice under a settled law, though they are only vague and inappropriate metaphors when applied to the distribution of political powers.

ALL laws or usages which favor one class of people to the disadvantage of others, which check the efforts of any part of the community in pursuit of their own good, are violations of the fundamental principles of public policy.

ELECT a legislature sufficiently free from political, partisan, and social affiliation as to endeavor to harmonize the interests of Capital and Labor, and remove the imperfect conception of justice, righteousness, equity, and humanity. Let it pass laws that regulate but do not enslave.

THE interests and prosperity of the country are dependent upon the producing class, and the leaders of politics must account to these producers for their actions. They are "the masses," the majority of our citizens, and, therefore, no other class is entitled to so much consideration at the hands of legislation.

IT is well enough to cry "Liberty!" when slavery rages, but the crying will not bring it. Let the liberty that is acclaimed, the freedom that is lauded, and the injustice that is asserted be subjected to the test of analysis, so that it may be really known what principles enter into their composition.

CAPITALISTS continue to apply all their energies to the acquisition of wealth, utterly mindless in most cases of any idea as to what has given it to them. Let us reason together: The toiler acknowledges that he cannot compel capital to bend to his terms, but capital must not forget that if there is a real cause of dissatisfaction which grows out of injustice, the sooner justice is done the less serious will be the reckoning.

THERE is really no conflict between Capital and Labor, but there is a conflict between the representatives of Capital and Labor. Therefore, since there is a despotism of Capital over Labor through representatives, the laborers should send to the front as their representatives such political parties as shall make it their business to frame laws in the interests of Labor, and these parties shall not allow themselves to be used as puppets to be so manipulated as to keep others in place and power. Why should the rich alone be represented?

> "If there be some weaker one,
> Give me strength to help him on;
> If a blinder soul there be,
> Let me guide him nearer Thee."

SLAVERY of the body should no longer be possible. The verdict of the twentieth century proclaims it "far behind the age." One thing is evident to all, some great issue of vital importance must develop and be of sufficient magnitude and general importance to arouse the people from the indifference which has characterized the past.

IT is not for the best interests of wealth that it should heap up for itself more treasures of gold at the expense of poverty. On the contrary, it is to the true interest of the rich to render fullest justice and strictest equality to the demands of labor. The true interest of wealth consists in the general prosperity of the masses. Every person's best interest lies in the prosperity of his neighbor. The more prosperous the neighbor, the better patron he proves for the surplus commodities of the other. Our interests are so mutual that in the proportion in which we injure our neighbor we cripple our own interests and injure ourselves.

INDIVIDUAL benefit must not accrue from the acquisition of wealth at the expense or sacrifice of any general principle of justice, nor must Labor array itself in opposition to wealth. A bringing together of the two interests is what is desired; an assimilation, so that the same end shall be best subserved for both. Such a course will promote complete unity, harmony, and equality, and join both the capitalist and the laborer in a system of mutual and reciprocal interdependence. A union which will better the condition of the productive class and give it an independent position is a course consistent with freedom and justice.

ALL false systems will in time yield their sway to God's command, "Let there be light." Let there be a life full of justice, love, and wisdom. All over the face of creation, in the bosom of the earth and in the heart of man, is written, "Let there be light."

WE have but to question the earth whether or not, from its beginning onward through countless ages, it has obeyed the one great command, Progress, and we find that at no time since the earth was, has the law of progression been inverted and the world turned backward toward the point of beginning. Since that has not occurred in the past, we may safely conclude that it will not in the future, and that the present signs point toward Progress.

REWARD Labor in proportion to its excellence, else there will be no excellence to reward; the amount and quality of labor done by a man are related in some way or other to the amount of reward offered him. Skill as a universal rule is developed in proportion to wages; when we perform an action, we perform it in consequence of some motive of interest.

THE possibility of better wages is not a dream: Labor's grievance, being practical and not theoretical, will not be brushed aside; though it may be impossible to find a remedy at once, the grievance will nevertheless receive attention. Judgment for an evil thing, though many times delayed, is as sure as life or death.

THE toilers will not be treated like pigs and cattle much longer.

They now possess the secret of their own power—" The Union Label."

IT pays to treat the toilers as though they were of different stuff; it pays to have men in our employ in whom we have sufficient confidence to intrust our affairs. It pays to feel that the workman is not forced to accept an offer of employment without a just recompense.

" Behold, ye must not tread us down like slaves;
And ye shall not—and cannot."

THERE is not a horse throughout the world, able and willing to work, but has food and lodging, and feels satisfied. Poor workingmen, what are they with their scanty equipment, with the paring down of wages for the benefit of somebody's pocket and to the injury of somebody's soul !

THAT all men are born free and equal is the fundamental idea upon which our government is built; if the structure is not as yet perfect, the foundation is, and can never be destroyed; life, liberty, and the pursuit of happiness are not simply metaphors, but the lifeblood of American institutions.

WE have rid ourselves of chattel slavery; now let us dispose of commercial bondage. Patriotism must not be deafened by the mere cry of "Freedom and Justice," be they sounded ever so loudly. Foul things always seek for fairest names.

"Love thyself last. Look far and find the stranger
Who staggers 'neath his sin and his despair;
Go, lend a hand, and lead him out of danger,
To heights where he may see the world is fair."

WORKINGMEN, show your strength; a dwarf may dissemble, but dissimulation is not the part of a giant. No one is ever feared or respected if he be not strenuous. Be a man and you will be treated like a man. Appear as a coward and everyone will abuse you. What may appear far-fetched to-day will assume a serious aspect to-morrow. Do not lie supinely while the enemy binds you, hand and foot.

"To the victor belong the spoils," is a remnant of arbitrarily assumed authority unworthy of a government emanating from the whole people. The progress of human society consists in the better apportioning of wages of labor. The ideal of celestial justice is that it pays every man accurately what he has worked for, what he has earned, done, and deserved.

ACQUAINT the representatives of labor with your power. Have them recognize the fact that you have it in your command to elect a man who will legislate for you as well as for the capitalist, and by so doing do away with this insane denunciation of wealth by those who would stir up any kind of strife to become leaders, and who if possessed of the power of wealth would wield it more despotically than it is now exercised by those possessing it.

BECOME more than mere instruments of agitation, or an exposition of the injustice of Capital to Labor; be constructive in action. Arouse yourself to the importance of devoting sufficient time to preparing candidates who will at all times and under all circumstances work for the greatest good to the greatest number.

IN this way labor may hope to arise from its present position of degradation and sit side by side with capital in all public positions.

CEASE blaming others for results which you have it in your power to remedy, and do not expect those whose interests are at variance with yours to correct the evil for you.

THE energies of Labor reform should be directed to the main point from which benefit to itself must spring; therefore waste no time nor strength upon the minor issues, but concentrate all upon the one strategic point of organization.

"Workman of God! O lose not heart,
But learn what God is like;
And in the darkest battlefield
Thou shalt know where to strike."

JOIN hands in unity, and legislatures will bow in submission; instead of being the willing servants of corporate wealth they will be the servants of the people. 'Tis true that we have not the right to interfere with men, preventing them in their honest pursuits from acquiring as much wealth as they possibly can, but we have the right to legislate so as to prevent the rich from growing richer through a system of bondage that manifests itself through the poor growing proportionately poorer.

HORACE GREELEY said, " I stand here, friends, to urge that a new leaf be turned over—that the

Labor class, instead of fully waiting for better circumstances and better times, shall begin at once to consider and discuss the means of controlling circumstances and commanding times by study, calculation, foresight, union."

A Peep at Sociology.

THREE principles that tend to equalize conditions demand recognition: First, intelligence; second, patience; third, conscientious effort.

LABOR is the foundation of everything supporting the structure of civilization and the glittering dome of progress. On it are built the wonders of the world, the shrine where wealth comes to worship.

GOD, in his infinite wisdom, foreseeing the extremely important relation between Capital and Labor, ordained that there should be absolute diversity in nature. Among the marvels of his creation are some fitted by acquisitive ability, others by talent, to be respectively employer and employee. Of these classes the higher dignity should belong to Labor, since the artisan possesses the talent, the strength of mind, and the mechanical skill of the world.

GOD has seen fit to decree that there should be mutual dependence among us, just as he made the dull gray lichen cling to the rocks and draw its life from the cold stone which it gnaws into the very smallest fragments, so that the trees of the forest might take those particles up for nourishment.

THROUGH mutual dependence we find the planets in the heavens roll on in their orbits, balancing one with another; were the position of these planets to be changed or destroyed the whole face of heaven would likewise be changed or destroyed. So we find the necessity for mutual dependence between Capital and Labor.

> "He *prayeth best who loveth best*
> *All things, both great and small;*
> *For the dear God who loveth us,*
> *He made and loveth all.*"

THE wonderful precision of nature is well illustrated in a hive of bees. Nature through the queen, produces eighty thousand eggs, which when hatched constitute a community or swarm, comprising every order of bee necessary to the prosperity of the hive. This tiny insect illustrates the necessity of social inequality or division of labor, there being just so many honey gatherers, pollen gatherers, wax workers, nurses or feeders, drones and males. Each bee works in its peculiar line of labor according to its bent of disposition, yet all are mutually dependent one with the other and all to the common head. When the queen dies, they all die.

THERE will always be the necessity for some to plan and others to execute. Some must be like the large lakes to collect the waters, and others like the pipes that distribute the waters when collected. The stars are not all of the same brilliancy, nor are the mountains of the same altitude; the trees are not all of the same height, nor are the flowers alike in beauty or perfume; the waves of the ocean are not of just the same form, nor the blasts of the wind of the same strength; no two men look alike, act alike, think alike, nor live alike.

FOR such and kindred reasons we must have division in labor; the nearest approach we may hope to attain to social equality is in the receiving of value for value given, "A fair day's wages for a fair day's work."

CAPITAL legitimately employed is entitled to the protection of the laborer and to the protection of the law. Labor honestly performed is entitled to its full reward, that the conditions surrounding the laborer shall be consistent with the demands of modern civilization. Each owes the other a solemn duty.

ANDREW CARNEGIE, in a speech to the men at Homestead, said: "Labor, capital, and business ability are the three legs of a three-legged stool; neither is first, neither is second, neither is third. There is

no precedence, all being equally necessary. He who would sow discord
among the three is an enemy of all."

W. H. MALLOCK, in "Social
Equality," points out the necessity
of "social inequality" thus: "To
what cause in human nature is the
gradation of labor due? What,
when some men are shepherds, or
carters, or dock laborers, is the cause
of other men being skilled mechanics,
or electricians, or engineers, or chem-
ists? Why, when on their labors
some men expend so little thought,
do others expend so much work?
. . . The human character is so
constituted that without the desire
of this irregularity as a motive, the
higher forms of skill, or even of ap-
plication, are wholly unproducible.
It is not that men would not choose

to produce them, but they could **not** produce them. Just as a woman is the proper cause of a man falling in love, so the inequality spoken of is the proper cause of a man's developing skill in labor; and to say that any other cause than this could make him develop it would be about as true as to say that, in the absence of a woman, he would be made to fall in love by the tablecloth. . . .

"WITHOUT division of labor not a single train could run, not a single newspaper could be printed. If articles of value could be produced without it at all, they would be the rare luxuries of the rich, not the necessaries and comforts of the poor. More hands are concerned in producing a yard of printed cotton than in producing a yard of tapestry.

The more popular, the more essentially democratic is the product, the more is division of labor invoked in the production. . . . Nor can anyone urge that this present state of affairs is due to our social arrangements, and not to human nature. For if human nature were ever really capable of being motived to skilled production by anything but the desire for inequality, no social arrangements could tend so strongly as ours do to bring that capacity to the surface. It is the notorious wish and endeavor of all modern employers to secure skilled labor at as cheap a rate as possible. If, therefore, skilled labor can be really motived by benevolence, or by any other motive except the desire for inequality, the laborers of today have every facility afforded them for making the fact apparent. They have only to do willingly the very thing which their employers would make them do, and which they, with a vigor that increases every day, declare they will never dream of doing."

WORKINGMEN or any class of toilers, authors, sculptors, scientists, artists, or inventors, will exert themselves little, unless they have a motive to exert themselves much; unequal reward is the cause of unequal labor. Lower kinds of labor are produced by a low rate of wages, higher kinds of labor by a high rate. This is no arbitrary valuation, but a law of nature.

CAPITAL cannot exist entirely divorced from Labor, Labor cannot flourish without Capital.

THE truth of this is well illustrated in the life of a tree, where the upper branches and twigs are dependent upon the same source for its controlling life current as are the parts nearest the base. No single branch can maintain its life independent of the rest. Each must work in harmony with the other.

THIS peep into sociology, if such it can be termed, is taken because it is not my intention to picture the toiler as always in the right and the employer always in the wrong. I desire to be the friend of all men, not a mischief breeder; to harmonize both Capital and Labor; to create and cement a lasting friendship; to make every man feel his importance, that he is the equal of any man if he so elects to be.

LABOR is honorable. Christ dignified Labor. He himself lived a hard and laborious life, and chose his immediate disciples from among the working people. God often called men to places of dignity and eminence when they were busy in the honest employment of an obscure vocation. Saul was seeking his father's asses and David keeping his father's sheep when called to the kingdom. The shepherds were feeding their flocks when they had the glorious revelation of the Nativity. "God never encourages idleness, and despises not persons in the meanest employments." "The humblest life may be noble, while that of the most powerful monarch may be contemptible."

THE man who cheerfully plunges into labor and sustains his part well is deserving of the highest respect.

All callings are alike honorable, if pursued with an honorable spirit; it is the vicious sentiment of the heart that degrades, the intention carried into the work, not the work itself.

"*This is the gospel of Labor, ring it ye bells of*
    the kirk—
The Lord of love came down from above to live
    with men who work—
This is the rose that he planted, here in the
    thorn-cursed soil;
Heaven is blessed with perfect rest, but the bless-
    ing of earth is toil."

THE talent that will make a good lawyer runs to waste if diverted into an attempt to make a skilled physician. A man who is wrapped up in mechanics cannot succeed as a clerk, for every drop of blood and all his brain cells enter a perpetual protest against the misuse of his faculties. Millet throws upon a bit of canvas "The

Man with the Hoe," and Markham writes a poem upon it. Had each attempted the other's task, both would have remained in obscurity. As it was, each working in his appointed field—the one in art, the other in literature—has evolved a thought which has caught the conscience of the world and moved it to its profoundest depths.

ABRAHAM LINCOLN in his early days was a workingman, and never quite rid himself of the idea that he was still a hewer of wood. He often expressed the belief that some day he would go back to his farm and earn his daily bread by the work that his hands found to do.

RECOGNIZING Labor as honorable, we must also admit the fact that Labor has grown tired of suffering, the eating of dry bread, and the sleeping on hard beds. Labor desires to rise above these conditions and go forward. Labor wants to be an instrument of justice, a terror to crime, and an aid to education. Labor appreciates that a stream cannot rise higher than its source, and that law is circumscribed by its execution.

LABOR'S ambition is not for a degraded spirit, an injured body; living in barren and poorly furnished rooms, dressing meanly, eating coarse and inferior food; being starved, cramped, wounded, and dejected. Labor knows that " Poverty " has no merit; that, " Hard Times " do not always bring forth and develop the best qualities; that a plant deprived of air, earth, water, and sunshine will not and cannot flourish and be healthy and fruitful.

LABOR must suffer disastrous results unless organized to protect and promote its interests; a man must always live by his work, and his wages must at least be sufficient to maintain him; alone, man is weak, and only strong enough in combination to demand that the fruits of industry should be insured and proportioned as much as possible to the benefits which it produces; the methods of production are subjects which embrace the happiness and welfare of the wage-earner; beneath the surface of production lie the causes of the heartaches and the tears of a destitute, helpless multitude, the victims of monopolistic greed.

LABOR knows from experience that long hours of hard manual labor destroy the mental appetite and unfit one for enlightenment or education. If then the toilers continue to allow themselves to be coerced and restricted, they must denounce the inalienable rights of organization and submit to degradation and slavery.

THE following advice of Wendell Phillips is well expressed: "If you want power in this country, if you want to make yourselves felt, if you do not want your children to wait

long years before they have the
bread on the table they ought to
have, the opportunities in life they
ought to have, write on your banner
so that every political trimmer can
read it, 'We never forget.' If you
launch the arrow of sarcasm at labor,
we never forget; if there is a division in Congress, and you throw your
vote on the wrong scale, we never
forget. You may go down on your
knees and say, 'I am sorry I did the
act,' and we will say, 'It will avail
you in heaven, but on this side of the
grave, Never.'"

ORGANIZED Labor, in its battle
for justice, must utilize every legitimate weapon to make its influence
felt, and consistently strive to uphold
its friends and refuse to strengthen
its enemies. Where a merchant

shows by his actions that he is friendly to the cause, he is entitled to the laboring man's patronage. The workingmen and the merchants therefore should join together for the improvement of the condition of all, and put it beyond the power of unscrupulous employers to fatten on the heart's blood of helpless individuals. They should stand forth in all their might and demand that this scandal, this crime of unfair wages, be swept from our land. We should make civilization the friend of the poor, and not dupe the poor into making themselves the enemies of civilization.

JUSTICE was ordained from the foundation of the world and will last with the world and longer; the righteous and the noble will gain the victory in the struggle. The principles which make it possible for one man to control a dozen horses possessed of a thousand times his own strength, is the power of knowledge over ignorance. The horses are ignorant of their real power and yield obediently to the command of assumed authority, so the mass of laborers, ignorant of their power, yield obedience to the assumption of a superior intellect.

AWAKE, educate, agitate, act! The rank and file have too long marched to the measure of silver-tongued oratory, the denunciation of our country and its institutions. Why be mere automata with no wills of your own? Why countenance party leaders who have built up theories which lack the support of science and principle, who put before you issues colored and trimmed to suit their prejudices and calculated only to arouse opposition?

LET all unite. Labor shall no longer be the scapegoat of the sins of the people. Unity will bring about a thorough expression of humanity. The crown of thorns on the brow of Labor will shine like a diadem. Employers of Labor will not only approve of unity, but will gladly urge all employers to join hands. Organized capital will be satisfied to recognize organized Labor and treat with it on terms of equality and fairness. It is necessary, therefore, that the governing power of Labor be vested in a federation of trade, with the necessary control to compel all craftsmen into harmonious action, so that no antagonism may arise to divert the tendency to unity of purpose.

EACH local union has its place, but the national and international organizations cover the whole field and represent the glorious work in which all are engaged. Every workman who is worthy of his calling is the comrade of every other toiler, and quarrels for precedence and invidious claims of superiority are simply so much aid and comfort given to the enemy.

IT is well enough for a workingman to take pride in the particular union to which he belongs, and to do all that his courage may suggest to make its record clear and brilliant, but he has no right to ignore the fact that his little local is part of the army as a whole, and that every toiler, from whatever place he hails, and whatever trade he follows, has a claim on his sympathy and co-operation. If he fails to give both, and give them generously, he is not a citizen of the best type.

CITIZENS, give this movement approval and support. It was conceived in a spirit of justice and fairness and was born of the necessities of our times. Thorough organization will render unto Capital what is Capital's, and unto Labor what is Labor's. Protection and profit to the former, employment and fair wages to the latter.

I *sometimes feel the thread of life is slender,*
  And soon with me the labor will be wrought;
Then grows my heart to other hearts more tender,
      The time is short."

POTTER PALMER, of Chicago, said: " For ten years I made as desperate a fight against organized Labor as was ever made by mortal man. It cost me considerably more than a million dollars to learn that there is no labor so skilled, so intelligent, so faithful as that which is governed by organizations whose officials are well balanced, level-headed men. I now employ none but organized Labor, and never have the least trouble, each believing that the one has no right to oppress the other."

Awake, Educate, Agitate, Act!

DEEDS, NOT WORDS.

THE toilers make themselves great or little according to their will. Act like sheep and you will be eaten by wolves. Conflict will, in all likelihood, determine the course of the world's history for ages hereafter, therefore the battle must be thought out and administered with the same precision and care as a blow of a pugilist is planned before it is delivered.

SURVEY yourself carefully; discover your weak and strong points; dissect yourself with the keen skill of a surgeon. Ask of yourself, What are you? Where are you going, and how are you to get there? The question is not what would you do were you somewhere else or some one else, but what you shall do now, here, as you are, and where you are.

MANY men are anxious to be of some force in the world, but lack the energy—the dynamo too small; the wires too tenuous; the current too weak.

EVERY toiler is like a vaporing teapot, full of steam, it is true, but with not enough force to lift the lid. Yet were the toilers to concentrate their entire steam in one boiler, the force would move the biggest stumbling-block ever placed in the pathway of progress. Were their power united in one dynamo, they could generate the principles that would demand recognition. Control the lever by concerted action, by a unification of the working classes. Knock a window into this problem large enough for the world to look inside and so give light upon the subject. Ambition should be your motto—ambition to think, to learn, to grow. Opportunities are all around; weak men wait for them, strong men make them. 'Tis not in our stars, but in ourselves that we are underlings.

WE are all screws in the great industrial machine of the world; when worn out each is mercilessly replaced by a new screw. If we are in skill at the top and in wages at the bottom, it is because we have no special direction of revolution.

WE move in accordance with immutable law, not chance—the product and result of everlastingly pressing on for supremacy.

"As we sow, so we reap."

PROVIDENCE owes spite to no one. Nature's laws are operated in co-operation with strong heroic endeavor.

CHANCE will not clothe us, feed us, nor house us. Accident will not soften the heavy hands of poverty, sweeten the cup of bitterness, nor lighten the burden of life; it merely sends the breeze to sail the ship of Labor into the harbor of safety. Should the pilot slumber at the helm, the very winds that would otherwise carry the ship to port will dash it on the shoals. Let the steersman's part be vigilance—blow it rough or smooth. Stick together as one man till the last bar is crossed. To lose faith in oneself is more deplorable. than the loss of capital. You can and will succeed though others do not believe in you, but never when you do not believe in yourself. Disbelief and irresolution never won a victory.

"BEHOLD, ye shall grow wiser or ye shall die." Let each true man stand to his work in the ship; turn the prow in the direction of actual, living, moving principles of freedom and justice.

> "Is thy cruse of comfort wasting?
> Rise and share it with another,
> And through all the years of famine
> It shall serve thee and thy brother.
> Is thy burden hard and heavy?
> Do thy steps drag heavily?
> Help to bear thy brother's burden:
> God will bear both it and thee."

EVERY individual is but one of the millions who live on the earth, each of whom feels the innate sentiment of self right. Those exercising their selfish ideas. should be restrained and compelled to harmonize their interest with that of others, so that no one person may interfere with any other.

LET Labor but once learn this lesson and strike at the business counter of the Non-Union stores, and it will carry with it an influence and example that no opposition can withstand.

THE corner stone of the foundation upon which humanity is to rest must consist of perfect individual justice, which will not be inconsistent or at war with perfect collective justice.

IF a man longs for light, let him go where the light can reach him, and not sit in a dark corner where only ghastly shadows of hell and poverty lurk. Let him join a Union; attend all its meetings; purchase Union-made productions.

LET us have deeds, not words. Performances are better than promises, for exuberant assurances are cheap. Wake up from this apathy of despair into which you have fallen, and sharpen your intellect while struggling for supremacy.

DON'T wait for something to turn up, but pitch in and turn something up. It is well and good to strike while the iron is hot, but it is a thousand times better to make the iron hot by striking it, and when you do strike come down with a sledgehammer-like blow that will mean "The Union Label on everything."

IF it is the end that crowns your undertakings, it is the beginning that gives it form. To reach the top you must first begin at the bottom.

TAKE a lesson from the two farmers living side by side, neighbor to neighbor, both lovers of good horse flesh; one fond of buying every fine specimen, the other bent upon raising his own stock.

ONE day the farmer with his clumsy tribe hitched up his team to a big supply of the products of the earth, and as he gave the word "Go," all the horses pulled together and the load moved slowly but surely. The other farmer looked on with a smile of derision and soliloquized,

"Now, I'll just give him a start of half a mile, then I'll hitch my racers and beat my neighbor into market." True to his word, he gave the farmer a good start and then hitched up his team and let them go. For a time they made rapid strides, when suddenly a rut was encountered. The horses commenced to pull counter to each other; one shied this way, the other that. The load would not yield. The farmer fretted and cursed, and, as he puffed and swore, he beheld his neighbor returning. "Well, I'll be gol darned," said he; "here I have been for years collecting the finest horse flesh to be had, and when it comes to a show down with that clumsy tribe, I am not in it. Hey, there, neighbor! How did you manage to get back so quick?"

"EASILY explained," says his neighbor. "My horses all pull together; yer see, this hyar horse is the father of the team, the other is the mother, and the other two are the children. Now, I've kept this hyar family together and trained them so they'll never pull against the tide—always with it."

LABORING man, that is the secret of the lesson you must learn. Open the book page by page, read it chapter after chapter. No one can read it for you as you can yourself, no one can feel like you, think like you, or be affected just as you are affected. Pull together. On the battlefield, when the mettle of every man is tested, and when the cause is worth the sacrifice made to win, it is fatal to victory if the different branches of the trade refuse to stand shoulder to shoulder and face a common foe.

THERE are times when your eyes will ache, your head grow dizzy, your energy dribble away. Arouse yourself, determine to do your part, and so carry out the plans and accomplish the results you know are necessary. Honor your calling, and your calling will honor you.

NOTHING TO ARBITRATE?

THE Labor problem has been, and is at present much misunderstood. Many are inclined to believe that the strike, the boycott, the black list, are all that there is to the Labor question. But there is much more. It is the struggling of the masses for better conditions.

THE underlying factors of the Labor question had their origin so long ago that history gives no account of them. Far back in the ages certain tribes lived in Central Asia, east of the Caspian Sea. These tribes grew refined, intelligent, built boats, steered them with rudders and propelled them with oars. Then came the great feeling of unrest, which has followed the Aryan races to this moment, as traced through the Hindu, Greek, Latin, Celtic, Teutonic, and others.

WHEN the Roman Empire was at its highest, all the industries of the countries were performed by men who had been taken prisoners in battle and converted into slaves. Their lives and their comforts were considered matters of little consequence. The right of conquest permitted the conquered to be taken home, made slaves, and forced to labor that the master might eat, drink, and take his ease.

WHAT is to be done when from the cradle to the grave it is only a struggle for a crust of bread? Is it not human nature to rebel and seek improvement?

CHRISTOPHER COLUMBUS discovered to the inhabitants of the old world a new country, a land that was to be a haven of retreat, a land that would give them greater freedom and truer equality.

IT is self-evident that the one possible permanent remedy for the unsatisfactory condition that now environs the laboring and capitalistic world is through a better educated public mind regarding the natural relation of Capital and Labor.

THE toilers, as a rule, do not welcome a strike, but always prefer an adjustment of differences. But what are they to do when back comes a reply, "There is nothing to arbitrate"?

IF you were in the ranks of Labor and really believed that Capital was constantly gathering your earnings to itself, thereby rendering you more and more dependent upon the good graces of the rich for a livelihood, would you not strike?

THE cause of strikes is traceable far back to the past, when the old and well-known "iron law of wages" was in unmitigated force. The rate of wages in those days simply covered the absolute physical necessities of a man: his clothing, food, and shelter. Just a sufficient amount was granted to sustain the physical machine and keep it from depreciating in value.

RICARDO'S writings on wages may be summarized thus: "The natural price of labor is that price which is necessary to enable the laborers, one with another, to subsist, and to perpetuate their race without either increase or diminution. . . . The market price of labor is the price which is really paid for it, from the natural operation of the proportion of the supply to the demand."

WHEN the toilers are poorly housed, poorly clad, poorly fed, poorly educated, with just sufficient to keep them alive and in sufficiently good condition to continue to toil from day to day; when the grandeur of the civilization which the workers are helping to build becomes a mockery to them ; when they ask for a fairer adjustment of differences — back comes a reply, " Nothing to arbitrate." Is it not contrary to man's nature to rest quietly while he is being robbed, or while he thinks he is being robbed ?

THE retrospect of Labor conditions brings us back to child labor in England, when the mills were first established along the streams, and the wheels of the machinery were revolved by children from the almshouses, indentured and bound out at a fixed rate which compelled them to work sixteen hours a day, sick or well, frequently eating their dinner as they worked.

"NOTHING to arbitrate?" when these poor, helpless creatures were so poorly fed that they were often known to steal the food that had been thrown to the swine! "Nothing to arbitrate?" When being suspected of an intention of escaping from their cruelty and servitude, chains were fastened to their ankles and suspended from their hips! "Nothing to arbitrate?" when helpless children of a tender age worked all day long, and even walked to and from their work with the chains fastened to them?

"NOTHING to arbitrate?" when mothers in England, dehumanized and unmotherized, were made beasts of burden, carrying their children close to their breasts, while they themselves were hitched to coal cars and drew their burden through the underground mines!

HON. SEABORN WRIGHT, in the Georgia Legislature, defending the Anti-Child Bill, to protect children from manual labor, which was defeated, said, in substance: "I stood in the door of an humble cottage, shadowed by the factory's massive walls. The mistress of this home was the wife of a gallant Confederate soldier. They had seen better days. Death had kindly come to him, and he slept. The remorseless hand of necessity had driven the widow and her children out from the old homestead to the humble cottage. As I stood, the gates of the factory swung open, and, amid a hundred children, hers came forth. They were young children. The kindly walls of the nursery should have been around them. There was no spring in their steps, no light in their eyes; their cheeks were white, and I thought, standing in the presence of the children of that Confederate soldier, I would give every spindle and loom in the South to bring back the light to their eyes, and see the roses bloom

again upon their little cheeks. . . .
Last night I sat with my wife by
the fireside of our comfortable home.
I watched my eight-year-old boy lay
his head upon his mother's lap and
close his tired eyes in sleep, and I
thought, except for the goodness
of God, he might be numbered
among the thousand little toilers
in the mills of the South, through
the long hours of the night. And
then, with justice in my mind and
pity in my heart, I said, 'I will
do for the children of my people
what I would have them do for
mine.'"

READ the following two verses of
the "Cry of the Children," by Eliza-
beth Barrett Browning, depicting the
horrors and tortures of the children
driving the wheels of iron in dear

Old England, and then say, " Nothing to arbitrate!"

"True," say the children, " it may happen
  That we die before our time;
Little Alice died last year, her grave is shapen
  Like a snowball, in the rime.
We looked into the pit prepared to take her;
  Was no room for any work in the close clay!
From the sleep wherein she lieth none will wake
    her,
  Crying, ' Get up, little Alice! it is day!'
If you listen by that grave in sun and shower,
  With your ear down, little Alice never cries;
Could we see her face, be sure we would not
    know her,
  For the smile has time for growing in her eyes;
And merry go her moments, lulled and stilled in
  The shroud by the kirk-chime.
It is good when it happens," say the children,
  "That we die before our time."

   ·   ·   ·   ·   ·   ·

"For O," say the children, "we are weary,
  And we cannot run or leap;
If we cared for any meadows, it were merely
  To drop down in them and sleep.

Our knees tremble sorely in the stooping,
  We fall upon our faces, trying to go;
And underneath our heavy eyelids drooping,
  The reddest flower would look as pale as
    snow,
For all day we drag our burdens tiring
  Through the coal-dark underground;
Or, all day, we drive the wheels of iron
  In the factories, round and round."

PICTURE a poor widow slowly turning the corner of a street, and wiping away the tears that were fast chasing each other down her feeble cheek; follow her to her humble habitation; see her bestow a blessing upon three shivering, starving infants, and divide among them the few crumbs of bread which her day's labor had been able to procure. Bring before your mind the truth of this poor creature being driven insane by the thought of leaving those desolate children exposed to a world she had found so cold and pitiless. Picture men, women, and children daily picking the waste food from the refuse cans which decorate the streets, prior ·to their contents being thrown into the scavenger's cart—no vivid imagination or hallucination of the brain, but a true, unvarnished description seen by the naked eye.

WHAT shall we say of the foul, unhealthy homes, of the crowded alleys in which thousands upon thousands of our poor are lodged, of the evils caused by want, misery, starvation, cold, and disease; all suffering for the simplest demands of human nature, and with naught remaining to bury the dead?

EX-MAYOR ABRAM S. HEWitt, of New York City, speaking to a large assemblage, made comparison between rich and poor by stating: "Since 1840 our natural wealth has increased five times as fast as our population. Who shall say that, with the wonderful increase in wealth, there is not means in abundance to remove all the misery and all the evil conditions among the humble classes which at present are stains and sores on our body politic?"

"GOOD God! Is this the end to which we have been working all these centuries? Is this the result of our industrial development? Must our prosperity as a nation be purchased at such a staggering price?

"IF these terrible tenements, these overcrowded districts, these dark and foul dwelling places, and all the attending miseries, must go hand in hand with industry, then I pray God that every industrial center could be destroyed, as was Sodom and Gomorrah of old."

"Ill fares the land, to hastening ills a prey,
Where wealth accumulates, and men decay.
Princes and lords may flourish, or may fade,
A breath can make them as a breath has made;
But a bold peasantry, their country's pride,
When once destroyed, can never be supplied."

FOUR FIFTHS of the people of the world toil on year after year, and all the time see the other fifth reveling in the luxuries which the sweat of their brow has procured, and yet employers say, "Nothing to arbitrate!"

THOMAS CARLYLE, picturing the horrors and sufferings of the working class in England, said: "There are two millions of skillful workers sitting in the workhouses,

Poor-Law prisons, their hope of deliverance as yet small. Twelve hundred thousand workers in England alone are kept up as in a kind of horrid enchantment, glad to be imprisoned that they may not starve. . . .

"IN thrifty Scotland, in Glasgow or Edinburgh city, in their dark lanes, hidden from all but the eyes of God, there are scenes of woe and destitution and desolation, such as one may hope the sun never saw before in the most barbarous regions where men dwelt. . . . Not in sharp fits, but in a chronic gangrene of this kind is Scotland suffering.

"AT Stockport Assizes, a mother and a father are arraigned and found guilty of poisoning three of the children to defraud a 'burial society' of some £3 8s. due on the death of each child. . . . They, with their necessity and savagery, had been driven to do it. . . . A human mother and father had said to themselves, What shall we do to escape starvation? We are deep sunk here in our dark cellar, and help is far."

WRITING further he says: "Day by day all men and cattle rose to labor, and night by night returned home weary to their several lairs. In wondrous dualism, then as now, lived nations of breathing men; alternating, in all ways, between Light and Dark, between Joy and Sorrow, between Rest and Toil, between Hope reaching high as Heaven and Fear deep as very Hell." Yet we hear, "Nothing to arbitrate!"

THE strong brute is tearing from the grasp of the weaker one the food it is eating, and the latter, too weak to remonstrate, relinquishes it with a whine. The eagle seizes from the fishhawk the trout the latter has taken from the deep, and in the gloomy pool the big fish eat the little ones. . . . "Nothing to arbitrate!"

THE miners in the anthracite regions of Pennsylvania live in huts and hovels; compelled to mine from three to four thousand pounds of coal for a ton, their requests and petitions for a hearing to remedy the awful wrongs from which they suffer are denied. No right to have a wage that will decently support themselves and their families? "Nothing to arbitrate!"

"NOTHING to arbitrate?" when they ask for the abolition of the truck store owned by the companies, at which they are compelled to trade; when they ask for a reduction in the price of powder from $2.75 to $1.50 a keg; when they ask for the observance of the law that they be paid in cash semimonthly; when they ask for an advance of 20 per cent in all wages less than $1.50 a day, an advance of 15 per cent in wages between $1.50 and $1.75 a day, and 10 per cent advance in wages above $1.75 per day?

"NOTHING to arbitrate?" when great corporations and railway companies pay their laborers from one to two dollars a day and vote their presidents royal salaries; when stock has been watered, interests distorted and perverted, and employees screwed down to the lowest possible notch in order to pay higher dividends?

"NOTHING to arbitrate?" When we consider that the car lines formerly operated over the Brooklyn Bridge, owned and controlled by the cities of New York and Brooklyn from 1883 to 1898, paid conductors two dollars and seventy-six cents for eight hours' work, now that the operation of that road has been turned over to the Brooklyn Rapid Transit Co. the same duties are seemingly balanced with value for value given, with a salary of two dollars for ten hours' work?

POOR and rich, governed and governing, cannot long live together under such conditions. If "free

competition" means that the more
cunning and adroit shall profit by
unfair bargains, enlightened laws
must make an end to all such
phases of free competition. It only
requires that all crafts should con-
solidate into a power that shall
influence every act of government
touching upon the laboring question.

"Ring out the grief that saps the mind,
For those that here we see no more;
Ring out the feud of rich and poor,
Ring in redress to all mankind."

WHEN we arrive at the advanced
stage of civilization we shall never
hear of strikes, and only occasion-
ally will there be need of arbitration.
All differences and disputes will be
settled in a practical, common sense,
and manly way. Good wages will

be the foundation of good order and of all good things.

IN the ancient world, Marcus Aurelius, in whose veins flowed the purest blood of the Roman aristocracy, and Epictetus, belonging by birth to the dregs of society, stood for essentially the same doctrine, "Justice and Equity." Marcus Aurelius to some extent caught his inspirations from the slave, and looked up to him as pupil to master. The whole teachings of Marcus Aurelius were that rank and station made no difference in human accountability; that the principles upon which a man acts, in whatever station, alone count. He believed that the right of every man was to be respected, and he aimed to be the ruler of a state in which there should be the same law for all, administered with regard to equal rights; to carry on a government which should respect, most of all, the freedom of all governed.

W HEN the National Founders' Association of Cleveland offered a bonus of two dollars a day to every Non-Union man who would go to work in their foundries and help break the power of the Molders' Union and defeat the men who went on a strike for an increase of ten cents per day in their wages, the "New York Times" condemned the action of that association and paid a glowing tribute to the cause of "True Unionism," saying: "When unions are managed by able and just-minded men, and respect their obligations and keep in good faith their agreement, when they cease the mischievous practice of striking and persisting in strikes to show their power, when reason moves and justice guides them, then they will cease to be part evil and part good and become, like any other established and beneficial social institution, a recognized good. For the full accomplishment of these ameliorations, we shall have to wait the slow growth of wisdom under the teaching of experience. The advance can be helped on by candor and fairness on the part of the employer."

JUST as soon as we have a people the majority of whom reason logically, think clearly, see their rights and intelligently strive to secure them, just so soon will we see the last of the colossal crimes committed

in the name of civilization. Meet
upon the plane of common justice,
and do unto others as you would
they should do unto you.

> "Every sower must one day reap
>   Fruit from the seed he has sown.
> How carefully, then, it becomes us to keep
>   A watchful eye on the seed, and seek
> To sow what is good, that we may not weep
>   To receive our own!"

"AWAKE, Educate, Agitate, and
Act!"

APPENDIX.

Appendix.

Factory Inspector's Fourteenth Annual Report.

New York, 1899, page 37.

NO subject has in recent years received a larger share of attention from students of industrial conditions, philanthropists, labor leaders, and legislators than that of "Tenement House Workshops," or, as they are commonly called, "Sweatshops." Our present "tenement-made articles" law is fashioned somewhat after the law of Massachusetts, the operation of which has given eminent satisfaction. Our amended tenement law went into effect September 1, 1899. Its operation thus far has clearly developed the fact that "sweating," or home manufacture, exists in Greater New York to an alarming extent.

173

Factory Inspector's Fourteenth Annual Report.

NEW YORK, 1899, page 50.

RIGHT in the very heart of the most enlightened, and one of the proudest cities of the earth—where civilization, and its attendant benefits, seems to be at its best—we have found some of the darkest spots of which the human mind can possibly conceive. From these hovels of human habitation, where men, women, and children of all ages herd together like so many cattle, some of our proudest and most respected citizens are drawing large dividends in the form of extortionate rentals.

Factory Inspector's Fourteenth Annual Report.

NEW YORK, 1899, page 55.

THE following detailed list of orders issued by the department, all of which have been fully complied with, will give but a slight idea of the amount of labor performed by the bureau in its work of looking after the condition of bakeshops during the past year:

REDUCED hours to sixty per week, 375; cease employing minor, 104; file certificates, 37; provide pipe and hood, or ventilate bakerooms, etc., 847; sanitary plumbing and drainage, 144; increase height of bakeroom to at least eight feet, 290; clean premises, remove coal, ashes, etc., 645; repair, and limewash or paint walls, ceilings, etc., 2,707; repair, scrape, oil floors, etc., or provide new floors, 1,053; remove beds, bedding, etc., and cease sleeping in bakerooms, etc., 222; keep dogs, chickens, etc., out of bakerooms, 118; provide wash sink, running water, flashing, remove casings, etc., 458; provide water-closets, remove water-closets from bake and storerooms, provide separate water-closets, etc., 173.

REPORT OF THE BUREAU OF LABOR STATISTICS.

CONNECTICUT, 1898, page 143.

HON. THEODORE ROOSEVELT, when he was a member of the New York State Assembly, spoke as follows on the bill to prohibit the making of cigars in tenement houses : "I have visited these pestholes personally, and I can assure you if smokers could only see how these cigars are made, we would not need any legislation against this system at all."

Union Label.

THERE are now 31 labels and three cards recognized by organized Labor. The unions using labels indorsed by the American Federation of Labor are :

Cigar Makers, Printers, Boot and Shoe Workers, Hatters, Wood Workers, Garment Workers, Tobacco Workers, Tailors, Molders, Horse Nail Makers, Salmon Fishermen, Bakers, Coopers, Tanners and Curriers, Teamsters, Leather Workers, Brewery Workers, Mattress Makers, Broom Makers, Carriage and Wagon Makers, Brick Makers, Bicycle Workers, Bottle Blowers, Brush Makers, Metal Polishers, Machinists, Horse Shoers, Piano Makers, Can Makers, Engravers, Ladies' Garment Workers, Musicians. The Clerks, Barbers, and Waiters have a card.

BUTTONS FOR UNION BARTENDERS.

"NEW YORK SUN," March 19, 1901.

THE Bartenders' Union has decided to adopt a button to be worn by its members when they are serving drinks. The buttons will be ready in a few days, and will be furnished to every union bartender. When this has been done notification of the fact is to be sent to the unions in other trades with the request that they will not purchase drinks from bartenders who do not wear a union button.

PRESIDENT GOMPERS' REPORT.

Twentieth Annual Convention American Federation of Labor.

LOUISVILLE, KY., December 6, 1900.

ON STRIKES.

THE strike of the anthracite miners of Pennsylvania involved over 150,000 persons. When this strike occurred but very few of the men were organized. The substantial victories and improvements obtained by the miners some years ago, together with a general improvement among the workers resulting from organized effort, had imbued the men in the anthracite regions with the fact that the burdens they were bearing and the injustices which were heaped upon them were no longer to be endured.

THE splendid contest and excellent results achieved are known to us all, and need not be recounted here. Sufficeth for us to say that the strike of the miners in Pennsylvania has done more to assist in wiping out misery and degradation than all other occurrences combined, and the record we have in regard to the bituminous miners' strike of 1897 may be set down here without hesitation; that the worst that the miners have had to undergo is passed, and in the future they will take their position shoulder to shoulder with their fellow-craftsmen, without the necessity of conflict, continually improving the conditions of themselves and those dependent upon them, and performing their share of the duties in the great and humane struggle of labor.

APPENDIX

On Compulsory Arbitration.

IT is strange how much men desire to compel other men to do by law. What we aim to achieve is freedom through organization. Arbitration is only possible when voluntary. It never can be successfully carried out unless the parties to a dispute or controversy are equals, or nearly equals, in power to protect and defend themselves, or to inflict injury upon the other.

THE more thoroughly the workers are organized in their local and national unions, and federated by common bond, policy, and polity, the better shall we be able to avert strikes and lockouts, secure conciliation, and, if necessary, arbitration; but it must be voluntary arbitration, or there should be no arbitration at all.

IT is our aim to avoid strikes; but I trust that the day will never come when the workers of our country will have so far lost their manhood and independence as to refuse to strike, regardless of the provocation, or to surrender their right to strike. We seek to prevent strikes; but we realize that the best means by which they can be averted is to be the better prepared for them. We endeavor to prevent strikes; but there are some conditions far worse than strikes, and among them is a demoralized, degraded, and debased manhood. Lest our attitude be misconstrued by silence, this convention should emphatically and without any ambiguity declare its position.

WORKMEN, BEWARE OF "COMPULSORY ARBITRATION."

The "New York Evening Journal," March 29, 1901, endorsed President Gompers' message, in the following well-expressed and pointed editorial:

"THERE is no doubt that the proper way of settling Labor troubles is through arbitration. There is no doubt that if very rich men were scrupulous or legislators honest, COMPULSORY arbitration, binding upon workmen and employers, would be desirable.

"But when you speak now of a BIG employer you mean, usually, a trust or some individual controlled by a trust.

"Trusts are corporations, without hearts or souls.

"Their rulers are men of violent prejudices, especially antipathetic toward Labor Unions.

"Everybody knows that of legislative machines or of legislating men the majority are subject to corruption by direct bribery or indirect influence.

"We support Mr. Samuel Gompers, head of the American Federation of Labor, in his opposition to compulsory arbitration.

"With compulsory arbitration on the statute books, we should very soon see the trusts bribing legislators or officials to appoint subservient arbitrators.

"Workmen, refusing to submit to bribed arbitrators, would be outside the pale of the law, and another disadvantage would be added to the conditions which confront them.

"It is difficult enough to win a strike now, however just the grievances, but at present strikes are at least lawful and recognized.

"They would be unlawful if persisted in after the compulsory arbitration law, and the right of men to strike would have to be fought out all over again.

"It is discouraging, but it must be said, that while money rules absolutely, as at present, men who want their rights must not put themselves at the mercy of any set of arbitrators whom money might subsequently buy."

APPENDIX

SECRETARY'S REPORT.

Twentieth Annual Convention American Federation of Labor.

THE effort to secure definite information as to gains and losses unions sustained by strikes during the past twelve months has been unusually successful. While the information does not cover all the strikes and lockouts, yet the results achieved by those reported show unusual results.

A CAREFUL compiling of the reports show that 688 strikes were officially noticed, involving 213,190 members. Of this number 455 were won, 74 compromised, 106 lost, and 53 pending. Number of persons benefited were 217,493, and 11,257 did not receive a substantial benefit.

SECRETARY'S REPORT.

NAME.	No. of strikes won.	No. of strikes compromised.	Strikes pending	No. of strikes lost.
A. F. of L.	40	14	15	6
Allied Metal Mechanics.	......	......	......	......
Bakers.	3	......	......	......
Barbers.	......	......	......	......
Blacksmiths.	......	......	......	......
Boiler Makers.	49	3	......	4

NAME.	No. of strikes won.	No. of strikes compromised.	Strikes pending	No. of strikes lost.
Bookbinders............	3	......	......	2
Boot and Shoe Workers .	3	1	......	1
Brewery Workers........	......	......	......	......
Brick Makers	3	......	2	
Broom Makers..........	6	......	......	......
Carpenters, Brotherhood.	......	......	......	......
Carpenters, Amal. Soc...	10	1	......	1
Carriage Makers	4	......	......	2
Carvers, Wood.........	10	3	......	2
Cigar Makers..........	92	10	......	20
Clerks.................	2	......	......	......
Coopers...............	15	3	3	7
Core Makers...........	......	......	......	......
Curtain Oper., Lace.....	......	......	1	......
Drivers, Team.........	12	2	......	3
Electrical Workers......	......	......	......	......
Engineers, Coal Hoisting	1	......	......	......
Engineers, Steam.......	5	......	5	......
Engineers, Amal. Soc...	......	......	......	......
Engravers, Watch Case..	3	......	1	......
Firemen................	3	1	......	1
Fitters and Helpers, Steam	......	1	......	2
Garment Workers, United	......	......	2	......
Garment Workers, Ladies'	2	......	......	4
Glass Bottle Blowers	......	......	......	......
Glass Workers, National.	......	......	......	......
Granite Cutters........	1	......	......	......
Hatters, United	1	1	......	......
Horse Shoers...........	4	4	......	......
H. R. E. I. A. & B. L..	14	......	......	......
Jewelry Workers........	......	......	......	1
Laborers, Building......	......	......	......	......
Lathers................	......	......	......	......
Leather Workers........	10	......	......	1
Longshoremen..........	9	2	......	1

NAME.	No. of strikes won.	No. of strikes compromised.	Strikes pending	No. of strikes lost.
Machinists...............	24	9	......	5
Meat Cutters.............	......	......	2	......
Metal Polishers.........	14	2	......	1
Metal Workers, Sheet....	......	......	......	......
Metal Workers, United...	......	......	1	......
Mine Workers, United...	......	......	......	......
Molders, Iron..........	8	1	8	15
Musicians..............	......	......	......	......
Oil Workers............	......	......	......	......
Painters...............	14	2	......	2
Paper Makers...........	......	......	......	......
Pattern Makers.........	4	1	3	2
Plumbers..............	......	......	......	......
Plate Printers..........	1	......	......	......
Pressmen, Printing......	15	5	......	......
Potters, Operative.......	1	......	......	......
Railway Employees, Street	6	......	1	3
Railway Trackmen.......	......	......	......	......
Spinners, Mule.........	2	......	......	......
Stage Employees........	3	......	4	......
Stove Mounters.........	4	1	......	1
Tailors................	21	2	......	3
Textile Workers........	......	......	......	......
Tile Layers............	......	......	......	......
Tin Plate Workers......	......	......	......	......
Tobacco Workers.......	......	......	1	......
Trunk and Bag Workers.	......	1	1	......
Typographical Union ...	7	......	......	11
Upholsterers...........	8	4	......	2
Weavers, Elastic Web...	2	......	......	......
Weavers, Wire.........	......	......	1	......
Wood Workers.........	16	......	3	2
Total............	455	74	53	106

**ARRANGED AND PRINTED AT
THE CHELTENHAM PRESS
NEW YORK**

The Successful Man of Business

SECOND EDITION.   BRENTANO'S, NEW YORK, 1900

By BENJAMIN WOOD

12mo.   Cloth.   208 Pages.   Price, $1.00

A book outlining the broad principles upon which all permanent business success is grounded. No branch of the subject is neglected

EXTRACTS FROM REVIEWS

By Prominent Representative Publications.

The endeavor to combine poetic fancies with the practical lessons of commercial life is rather uncommon, and we follow Mr. Benjamin Wood in his volume, " The Successful Man of Business," as we might a pioneer into new regions of literature.—*New York Sun*, March 18, 1899.

The thousands who desire commercial success ought to make an eager public for " The Successful Man of Business."—*The Churchman*, New York, Feb. 3, 1900.

I have read " The Successful Man of Business " with the greatest interest, and shall place it where it will be accessible to the young men of the University.—DAVID STARR JORDAN, President Stanford University, Palo Alto, Cal.

We sincerely wish that every young man in the English-speaking world would obtain, study, and heed the counsels given by Mr. Wood in his volume, " The Successful Man of Business."—*Leslie's Weekly*, New York, Jan. 13, 1900.

Mr. Wood writes in a graceful, even poetic, way and not infrequently condenses his advice into a terse and epigrammatic phrase that sticks tenaciously in the memory.—*Picayune*, New Orleans, June 3, 1900.

The hard cold facts that are presented by Mr. Wood are robbed of sterility by the author's easy conversational style.   It is a book that can be read again and again with pleasure as well as profit.—*Republican*, Denver, June 3, 1900.

The author handles his question with a care and ease of manner born of long and intimate knowledge of stable business methods.—*Democrat*, Chicago, June 9, 1900.

The book is almost certain to retain the attention of any reader, although this is not what would be expected from a book with this title. —*Times*, Hartford, Sept. 20, 1900.

A book of high and inspiring idealism applied to the hardest kind of reality with the most unflinching realism. — *Evangelist*, New York, Oct. 18, 1900.

"The Successful Man of Business " is appropriate in sentiment and inspiring to fine thoughts.—*Journal of Education*, Boston, Feb. 15, 1900.

" The Successful Man of Business " is a good book to place in the hands of boys and young men who are just entering upon a life career. —*Review*, Boston, Jan. 20, 1900

The author seeks to point the way for energetic men who have a high conception of the duties of a business man.—*San Francisco Chronicle*, March 31, 1899.

The author has gone into the inner lives of men who have made a success and sought out those qualities that have led to supremacy.—*San Francisco Call*, April 9, 1899.

It is a book from which every young man can gain much.—*San Francisco News Letter*, Nov. 10, 1900.

The book is so fascinating that the reader who takes it up will read every chapter.—*Palladium*, New Haven, June 13, 1900.

The author lays down certain fundamental principles which will be recognized by every person of discernment as constituting the corner stone of advancement.—*Herald*, Baltimore, May 27, 1900.

The author, filled with his subject, carries great enthusiasm into his task, and it might be hoped that every young man will secure a copy of the book and give it serious study.—*North American*, Philadelphia, June 1, 1900.

The chapter called "Solid Facts" is commendable. If it were read to every young man, it would turn the lazy ones' thoughts to other channels and make of the earnest ones model men of business.—*Journal*, Albany, June 2, 1900.

There is nothing about this book to call forth aught but praise, for it is a cleverly gotten up work.—*Item*, New Orleans, June 3, 1900.

It is in the main intensely practical and filled with common sense advice.—*Record*, Chicago, June 2, 1900.

SD - #0043 - 291123 - C0 - 229/152/10 - PB - 9780259531104 - Gloss Lamination